www.psychmechanics.com

Exploring the forces that shape the human psyche

www.psychmechanics.com

Contents

Introduction

It doesn't take an expert to know that depression today is one of the most common psychological issues of people throughout the globe. Though it's more common in some cultures than in others, more people are depressed today than were, say, fifty years ago.

Despite its omnipresence, depression is also one of the most misunderstood topics in the fields of psychology and psychiatry. No wonder laymen are even more confused.

Do a quick research on depression on the internet and you'll see so many differing opinions and theories. You can spend hours and still end up confused, more than ever.

You probably chose to read this book because you're fed up with all the useless information that you may have come across that failed to help you get rid of depression.

On one hand we have people saying that depression is a temporary phase of sadness that passes away like clouds in the sky and on the other hand we have people who claim depression is the result of a chemical imbalance in the brain.

As you'll find out, both are wrong.

Whether you want to help yourself or someone you care about get over depression, or are simply interested in understanding depression, this book will of immense help even if you have no prior knowledge of psychology.

Wherever I felt that a concept needed explaining for a reader new to psychology, I have done so.

To get the most out of this book, it's highly recommended that you don't skim through it or speed-read it but focus, analyze, and reflect on each concept presented

What depression looks like

It's common wisdom that the first step to conquering anything is to understand it.

The biggest reason why many people find it hard to deal with their emotional problems, be it depression or anything else, is simply a lack of proper understanding of their emotional problems.

If there's a glitch in your computer, you can troubleshoot it and fix it. If your car breaks down, you can easily identify and solve the problem. If you get a physical wound you can wash it, apply antiseptic and cover it with a bandage.

All of the above problems had one thing in common- they were physically observable- you could see them happening with your eyes. And because you could *see* what went wrong, you were able to fix it.

Since psychological phenomena can't be observed physically that's why they're hard to understand and resolve.

I bet if people could see, literally see, how their emotions change, they would have a much easier time solving their emotional problems.

For instance, if a purple cloud appeared in front of people that changed color whenever they felt different emotions, I'm sure a lot of people would be able to deal with their emotional problems- for they would be able to see when their emotions and moods change and what causes them to change.

But reality is much more complicated than that. Bad moods and depression catch us off guard and we usually have no idea why we feel the way we feel.

So, there's no way to know what depression looks like and this puts us at a disadvantage.

We don't know how to identify it. We don't know where it comes from and how we're engulfed by it. We can only experience and feel it, often and unfortunately, when we're deep under its grip.

Ergo so much confusion and misunderstanding around depression. Even people who're not really depressed sometimes think they are and those who are sometimes think they're not.

How do we identify depression then?

How can we be certain that we're depressed so that we may begin to take proper steps to overcome it?

We'll consider the cases of three made up characters who suffer from depression- Mark, Shane, and Anna.

No longer able to handle their painful feelings, they decided to post their issues on an online forum dedicated to helping people with psychological problems.

Let's take a look at what they wrote...

"Hi, I'm Mark. I'm 27 and facing the hardest time of my life right now. I am well-educated and work at an insurance company. The money is good but the job is a dead end. I hate having to waste hours each day doing meaningless tasks. I've been depressed for months now. It's sucking the life out of me. I can't take it anymore."

....

"I'm Shane, an 18 year old student. I'm shy and hence find it very difficult to interact with people. I have no friends since I avoid social interactions as much as I can. I feel very sad, lonely

and depressed. I've been depressed ever since I joined college about a year ago."

....

"This is Anna, a 24-year-old fashion designer. I was in a long-term relationship with a guy and we recently broke up after 5 years. I really loved him and still do but I know I can't have him back. I lie alone in bed all day trying to make sense of what happened and cry all night."

....

Even though these are fictional characters, such cases of depression are commonplace and thousands of people might be feeling exactly the same right now as you're reading this.

Keep in mind that depression cases can be very varied and much more complicated in nature than the examples that I've stated above.

To aid understanding, I've selected relatively less complicated cases. But the principles that underlie both simple and complex cases of depression are the same.

Whatever the reason behind depression, it's always accompanied by painful feelings of sadness, emptiness, and hopelessness. You've got no energy to do anything and even lose interest in the activities that you used to enjoy prior to your depression.

Sometimes, depressed people also feel suicidal and end up actually doing the deed.

What are emotions for anyway?

Now that we know how Mark, Shane, and Anna are feeling the next logical question is *why*?

Before I can answer that question, I need to tell you a little something about emotions and feelings in general.

Ever wondered why we feel emotions? What are they for anyway?

Well, the purpose of emotions- all emotions- is to motivate us to take action. That's it. There's nothing more to it.

"What kind of actions?" you might ask.

Well, what kind of actions do you expect biological organisms to perform?

Of course, it's the actions that ensure their survival, reproduction, and well-being.

'Survival' and 'reproduction' are easy to understand but 'well-being' can be a tricky thing. What's well-being to you may not necessarily be well-being to me.

Let's put 'well-being' on the shelf for a while and discuss 'survival' and 'reproduction' first.

Many of our emotions have the end-goal of ensuring our survival and reproductive success.

Consider the example of the fear that you'd feel if you encountered a bear in a desolate forest.

What's the purpose of this fear?

To prepare you for fight or flight- both of which have the potential to save your life and prevent you from getting eaten.

What course of action you choose will be dependent on the context of the situation- the weapons that you might be carrying or find lying around, how big the bear is, etc.

5

Your mind will carry out the cost/benefit calculations of every feasible course of action and you'll arrive at a decision- you'll take on the bear or you'll run for your life.

See how useful fear was in this situation?

Had there been no fear, your body wouldn't have entered into the fight-or-flight mode and you probably would have had no idea what to do next.

There would have been no high levels of adrenaline rushing through your bloodstream, you wouldn't be breathing heavy and your heart wouldn't be beating faster to provide more oxygen to your muscles.

The emotion of fear motivated you to take action to increase your chances of survival. It set in motion a series of biological changes in your body to allow you to take action.

The emotion of hunger has the same use, only this time your 'emotion system' scans your body instead of the external environment.

When it finds that your body is depleted of nutrients, it has to alert you and motivate you to look for food. Had there been no hunger, you'd surely die of starvation.

Now let's talk about reproduction which isn't about the survival of your genes i.e. you but rather about their successful replication.

Successful replication of one's genes is the fundamental goal of biology. It's what moves life forward. It's what life is for, speaking purely from an evolutionary biological perspective.

The attraction that you feel when you meet an attractive member of the opposite sex has the goal of motivating you to have sex with that person, sooner or later.

This increases the likelihood of your reproductive success i.e. passing on your genes successfully to the next generation.

Survival and reproduction are the two most important goals of all living organisms, sometimes reproduction more than survival. There exist many species in nature who sacrifice their lives for the sake of reproduction.

So these two functions are central to understanding human psychology and cannot be overemphasized. Almost all our psychological mechanisms are designed around the critical functions of survival and reproduction.

It's time we brought 'well-being' to the table.

There are aspects of well-being that are common to all human beings. What that means is there are some life situations and conditions that ensure the well-being of every human being on this planet.

For example, approval and praise makes everyone happy. Success of any kind makes everyone happy. Feeling powerful, superior and in control is recipe for a feeling of well-being.

It's worthwhile to note here that the reason why all these things make us happy almost always has to do with their potential of increasing the odds of our survival and reproduction, but indirectly, as an ultimate effect.

For instance, approval and praise helps us remain in the good books of the members of our 'tribe' so that they may help us in times of need.

Now the tricky thing about well-being is that it can also vary from person to person, depending on what life experiences they've been through.

When our well-being is threatened, we feel the so-called negative emotions. These emotions exist to motivate us to restore our sense of well-being, just as hunger motivates us to restore our nutrients.

All the negative emotions and bad moods have the all-important purpose of motivating us to restore our sense of well-being.

Evolution certainly did not program humans to feel good all the time. So trying to feel good and happy all the time is an exercise in futility.

Negative emotions and bad feelings are equally important and useful. Just as positive emotions contribute to our survival, reproduction, and well-being so do negative emotions.

Depression is one such negative emotion, albeit much more severe than a mere, passing phase of bad mood or sadness.

Depression doesn't happen out of the blue just as fear doesn't happen out of the blue. For you to feel fear, your life situation should be threatening.

When your life situation is no longer threatening, fear disappears. If you encounter a cute, little squirrel instead of a dangerous bear in a jungle, you don't feel any fear.

Depression works in pretty much the same way.

What causes depression?

In order to understand how depression happens, you first need to grasp how mood swings happen. This is because depression can be viewed as an extreme case of a bad mood.

Why does your mood change and why is it so unpredictable?

It's surprising how many experts think that "the cause mood swings is a mystery". It's not. It's simple mathematics.

While it's true that your mood is controlled to a certain extent by your biological state (e.g. the foods you eat), most of the time, your good or bad mood is the result of the life situations you've been through.

Your 'moods system' is sensitive to a variety of cues that are directly or indirectly related to survival and reproduction.[1]

The way you're feeling at any given time is the resultant of the life experiences you've had up until that moment. How your mind interprets these experiences determines your mood.

If more good things happened to in the past five hours than bad things, then you'll feel good. If more bad things happened to you in the past five hours than good things, then you'll feel bad.

Of course, five hours is not some hard and fast rule here but only an example to make the idea clear.

Sometimes, however, one bad thing can be so bad that it can trump five good things. Or one good thing may be so good that it can trump five bad things.

The key point to understand is that your mind doesn't weigh all experiences equally. Some experiences matter to it more than the others.

Which way your mental scale tips to, good or bad, will determine your mood at any given moment.

So far, I've explained the *how* of good and bad moods, not the *why*. Let's discuss why mood swings happen:

Good moods basically motivate you to continue doing what you've been doing, not necessarily immediately. A good mood is a reward your mind gives you for doing what it considers the right thing.

Good moods are basically telling you...

"This is right. This is what you should be doing. This will enhance your survival/reproductive success/well-being."

Bad moods motivate you to avoid doing what you've been doing. A bad mood is a punishment to you from your mind for doing something that it doesn't consider right.

Bad moods are warning signals that tell you...

"This isn't right. This is not how things should be. This is not what you should be doing. This will hamper your survival/reproductive success/well-being."

Usually, when we're in a really good mood, we respond to the mind's message ("This is what you should be doing") by seeking activities and experiences that sustain or even increase our good feelings.

For example, the good feelings that we get on being successful makes us want to throw a party or give a treat. We eat, drink, and make merry to sustain or even increase our good feelings.

In general, good moods propel action. They motivate us to invest and take risks. "I'm not in the mood" is akin to saying "I don't want to take action."

On the other hand, when we get a bad mood, we're usually clueless about what to do next. Our mind's telling us, "Something is wrong. Make it go away" but we've no clue what's wrong.

It's not entirely our fault. Mood swings mostly happen unconsciously.

Say you're single and desperately looking for a relationship, and happen to visit a park one evening to watch the sunset. There, you notice a couple hanging out and embracing each other.

You might have felt good throughout the day, even while you were spending time in the park. But as soon as you reach home, you notice that your mood has changed for the worse. You have no idea why.

But if you rewind a little (I call this technique backtracking), you'll soon understand what went wrong. Your bad mood was triggered when you first noticed the couple.

In this case, your mind is essentially telling you, "You're single. This is not right."

That's how subtle mood swings can be. So if you want to get out of a bad mood you need to work on increasing your level of awareness.

You also need to learn to figure out what message your mind is trying to send you so that you can respond to it appropriately, because if you don't depression will be lurking around the corner.

In general, bad moods halt action. They motivate you to reflect on your life, figure out the faulty aspects, and choose an appropriate reparative action.

But since bad moods feel terrible, we're likely to ignore them or fix them by temporary means rather than listen to their message.

It's easier to run away from a bad mood and try to hide from it than face it, break it down, and understand it.

But how do we ignore bad moods?

Well, we humans are experts in ignoring bad moods. The most common way, however, is seeking pleasure.

Think about all the options that one has in today's easy and comfortable society to combat his or her bad moods.

I say easy and comfortable because there are no predators on the lookout for us (at least for most of us living in the industrialized parts of the world) and we don't have to risk our lives for getting food like our ancestors had to.

It's important to note that our psychological mechanisms were essentially designed for the Paleolithic times. We're stuck with Stone Age brains in concrete jungles.

Our ancestors must have had little trouble handling their bad moods because they hardly had any distraction and escapement options that today's society provides us.

Feeling bad? Eat a cake and forget about it. How about a pizza? Or maybe a drink? How about watching porn? How about playing video games? How about tripping on drugs?

There are endless ways we can make ourselves feel good *temporarily* when we're feeling bad. These options to short-circuit emotional pain were not available to our ancestors.

It may seem like the modern society has developed an ingenious way to cope with bad feelings. But you can rarely win against evolution.

The problem is that when we distract ourselves from bad moods by seeking short-term pleasure, bad moods don't go away permanently.

They come back with a greater intensity. Since you ignored the bad mood the first time, your mind is like, "Let me increase the intensity this time. Maybe he will listen this time."

If you still don't listen, the mind increases the intensity even more.

What happens if you still don't listen?

The mind increases the intensity further till it reaches a breaking point beyond which no further increasing of intensity is possible. It's at this point that you simply 'can't take it anymore'.

And lo and behold, depression sets in.

Depression enters the ring of your mind like a WWE wrestler and begins pounding on you like a madman seeking some kind of long-unsettled cosmic revenge.

Depression hits you when your mind increases the intensity of bad feelings to the highest level. The feelings are so severe that you're forced to finally acknowledge that 'something is indeed wrong' and try to seek help to end your terrible feelings.

Short-term pleasure no longer works.

What began as a mere bad mood has now turned into a demon. Every time you ignore your bad moods, you feed this demon that grows bigger and bigger till it finally takes over you.

Purpose of depression

To understand the purpose of depression you only need to look at what it does to you.

Depression reduces your energy level considerably to make sure you don't distract yourself with unnecessary activities and ignore your bad feelings again.

Your mind wants you to sit down and reflect on your life so that you may figure out what has gone wrong and make plans and strategies to solve your problem.

An especially hard problem requires deep thinking, contemplation, and observation that cannot be achieved if you're constantly exposed to distracting stimuli from the environment.

Interestingly, no matter how much you eat when you're depressed, your energy level remains low. It doesn't matter how much calories you stuff into your stomach, your mind simply refuses to cooperate. It forces you to stay at one place and re-assess your life.

Depression also makes you lose interest in the things that you liked doing before because this time solving your festered problem becomes a greater priority. Even your favorite activities become unnecessary distractions to your mind.

Depressed people prefer to stay alone. Consciously, they say they want to be left alone and subconsciously, the real aim is to reevaluate their life and devise strategies to solve their current life problem that has so gone out of hand.

A feeling of hopelessness is the key feature of depression that separates it from general sadness. Depressed people perceive their difficulties as overwhelming and beyond their control. They perceive their predicament as hopeless.[2]

This is primarily because the problem has gone out of hand and become complex thanks to continuous distraction attempts.

Depression is your mind's weapon of last resort to force your attention back to the critical problem at hand.

Research has shown that depression activates an area of the brain called the left ventrolateral prefrontal cortex (VLPFC), which is responsible for maintaining attention towards the target problem and eliminate other distractions.[3]

This is why depressed people are fixated on their seemingly unsolvable and hopeless problems and think of anything else.

Experiments reveal that neurons in the VLPFC must fire continuously to keep us on a task that requires our undivided attention and prevent us from getting sidetracked by irrelevant information.

For example, if you're reading this book with intense focus then neurons in your VLPFC are firing continuously.

Normally, it isn't easy to maintain attention on one task for long. Focusing intensely on something is a conscious, slow, tiresome, and distraction-prone process. Due to this the prefrontal cortex soon grows exhausted and gives out.

Depression is a way of bolstering our ability to pay continuous attention to a complex problem. The downcast mood and activation of the VLPFC are part of a coordinated system that exists for the purpose of effectively analyzing the complex life problem that triggered the depression.[4]

I think it's about time we defined depression:

Depression is an emotional state that motivates us to solve a problem that has negatively impacted our survival, reproductive success or general mental well-being. It usually begins as a bad mood which, when continually ignored, turns into depression.

Therefore, in order to end depression, all one has to do is to listen to the message that depression is sending and take actions to solve the underlying problem that's causing it.

As soon as the problem gets solved, depression will disappear because its purpose will have been served. It's not even necessary to solve the problem right away. Just by restoring hope, depression can be relieved.

Another angle from which to look at depression is stress. Depression is caused by adversity, a stressful life situation.

When you're working toward an important life goal and are unable to make any progress, this can lead to frustration which, in turn, can lead to stress.

Prolonged stress, from this perspective, then increases your risk of depression.

Depression, then, is a way your mind warns you that you're wasting your mental and other resources on activities that aren't bringing you any results.

Depression lowers your energy levels so that you don't continue doing the useless activities that you've been doing.

Instead, depression wants you to re-think your strategy and ruminate over alternate options.

This may result in you doubling your efforts toward reaching your goal or quitting and pursuing more worthwhile and attainable goals. Either way, depression's purpose is to solve your life problem.

The two types of depression

Psychologists typically categorize depression into two types-minor and major (called major depressive disorder, MDD).

Minor depression (like sadness) is seen as adaptive and functional while major depression is considered to be maladaptive and dysfunctional.

I, however, dislike the term maladaptive. Maladaptive behavior, in most cases, is just misunderstood adaptive behavior.

The key differentiating factor between minor and major depression is the degree of severity of the symptoms and the time period involved.

If your depression symptoms are severe and you've been experiencing them for long periods of time, then you have MDD. If, however, you're depressed because you lost money in the stock market couple of days ago, it is considered as mild depression.

The problem with this approach is that it ignores the more likely possibility that depression is part of a spectrum that has an innocuous low mood on one end and severe depression on the other. Instead, it views these two as separate conditions.

Add to this the fact that many symptoms of the minor and major depression overlap, to the point that psychologists have no way of knowing at which point a minor depression tips over to major depression.

It makes more sense to view minor and major depression as points on the depression scale, with low mood on the least severe end, mild depression in the middle, and MMD on the most severe end.

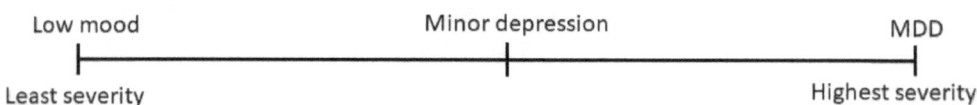

The depression scale

Just because a depression is severe doesn't mean it can't have causes that are usually behind minor depression.

Take, for example, the case of a person who lost money in the stock market. Psychiatrists will typically diagnose him with minor depression.

If he manages to find a way to recover his lost money quickly, his depression will end but if he doesn't, for a long period of time, he may well be diagnosed with major depression.

As mentioned earlier, the mind increases the intensity of signaling when you ignore its signals or are unable to resolve your problem.

MDD is nothing but your mind pushed to the limit. It stops everything and forces you to get help so that you can solve your problem. Therefore, it's not maladaptive even though it may appear to be so or have debilitating consequences.

Our evolved psychological mechanisms including depression, in general, tend to be adaptive or neutral rather than maladaptive.

Next, we discuss the traps depressed people commonly fall into, that are based largely on faulty thinking and popular myths.

Traps depressed people fall into

It's time we got back to Mark, Shane, and Anna- the characters I mentioned earlier who'd posted their problems related to depression on an online forum.

Let's review what Mark had posted in the forum:

"Hi I'm Mark. I'm 27 and facing the hardest time of my life right now. I am well-educated and work at an insurance company. The money is good but the job is a dead end. I hate having to waste hours each day doing meaningless tasks. I've been depressed for weeks now. It's sucking the life out of me. I can't take it anymore."

As you can see, Mark is depressed because he hates his job. It's natural to hate a job that doesn't pay you well. Less money means less resources and fewer resources can negatively impact your survival and reproductive success.

But Mark's job is paying him well. Hence, we can assume that his survival and reproductive success is not at risk. But something about his job surely isn't contributing to his well-being in some way.

When we move outside the realm of survival and reproduction, we have to look at a person's individual psychological makeup. Most probably, Mark's current job isn't able to satisfy an important psychological need of his.

What could that need possibly be?

If Mark figures out this important need of his that is not being met in his current job, then he can find a job that *does* satisfy it and his depression would end. This is the right course of action for Mark to take.

Let's see what people in the forum advised Mark to do...

Comment 1:

"Hey Mark, I know how you feel. I suggest you quit your job right away as it's clearly the source of your pain. Life's too short not to follow your passion. Do what you love."

It struck a deep chord within Mark and he took the bold step of quitting his job right away. But there was a little problem. He hadn't figured out his passion yet, let alone a way to make a living doing it.

After trying his hand at a few activities, he couldn't really decide what he wanted to do. His financial situation gradually worsened and took a toll on his health and relationships. He eventually settled for a job that was worse than his previous one.

Needless to say, he felt even more depressed. He had thought that quitting his job would land him into some magical land where wishes were granted and dreams fulfilled.

The "extreme step" trap

When we're depressed, the feelings are so painful and overwhelming that we're willing to do anything to come out of it. Instead of deeply analyzing our problem, we seek to jump out of it.

The pain is intolerable and even suicide sometimes becomes a viable option to end the pain.

In our desperation, we're likely to take actions that seem to promise quick and immediate results.

Depression is not asking you to solve your problem right away by taking risky, irrational, and heroic actions. It's just asking you to acknowledge that you have a problem, formulate a plan to overcome that problem, and begin working on that plan.

Had Mark understood this, he wouldn't have taken the risk of quitting his job right away. Before he could do that, he had to first figure out what he really wanted to do and how to make money doing that thing.

Many people fall prey to the 'get rich quick schemes' that show a ray of hope to the hopelessly depressed.

Depression isn't asking you to get rich now. It's asking to formulate a plan on getting rich and start working on it.

Here's what another commenter had to say...

Comment 2:

"Mark, be grateful for what you have. There are millions who're worse off than you. Think of the number of people dying from hunger in Africa every day. Thank the universe for being so generous with you."

It made a lot of sense to Mark. It was true. Perhaps he did need to learn practicing gratitude and be more thankful for the things that he'd taken for granted.

21

He thought about the starving people in Africa and realized that he indeed was living in paradise compared to them. His depression eased. But after some time, it returned.

He again forced himself to think about the starving people and his depression eased again. But it also returned again. And he again thought about the starving............ well, you know where we're going with this- nowhere.

The "gratitude" trap

To be clear, gratitude is indeed powerful and it does make us feel better. The problem, however, is that it's not a viable long-term solution.

If our problem is X and we think about Y to feel good, it doesn't mean X isn't there. You can distract your mind with gratitude all you want but the main problem remains unsolved and you're bound to feel depressed as soon as something reminds you of that problem.

Using gratitude to deal with depression is like saying, "The forest is lovely" when a tiger is about to leap on you. Yes, the forest is lovely but we're not concerned with that right now. All we're concerned with, in this moment, is to deal with the tiger- the big problem in front of us.

"Be grateful" is perhaps the most overrated and clichéd advice ever. You'll see it being repeated many times over because it's very effective in distracting us from the problem at hand.

Besides, there's no point really in trying to *force* a mental state like gratitude onto yourself. Either you are grateful in a given moment or you're not. Why force it artificially onto yourself just to prevent facing an uncomfortable underlying emotional state?

In truth, Mark didn't really care about who was living or dying in Africa. He just wanted to feel better temporarily because he had no idea how to deal with his depression.

You can think a thousand things that you're grateful for but if you don't fix that one underlying problem that's causing your depression, your depression won't go away.

How Mark ended his depression

Mark was depressed because his job was unsatisfying. His job was unsatisfying because it was not in line with one of his important psychological needs.

Mark was the youngest child in his family and was showered with lots of attention throughout his childhood.

When he was a teenager he was obsessed with wearing branded clothes and driving flashy cars. These activities helped him retain the attention that he'd gotten so used to in his childhood.

In college too, Mark tried his best to remain in the center of attention. He actively participated in debates, cultural and other extra-curricular activities. He loved giving speeches and jumped at every opportunity to basically stand out from the crowd, so that the crowd could pay attention to him.

After finishing his business studies, he worked as an assistant manager in an insurance company. He had to sit all day in front of a computer and talk to only a few people.

Clearly, Mark was no longer getting the kind of attention that he used to get. In the initial days at work, he felt a little uncomfortable. But gradually, the bad feeling grew and grew stronger since he was doing nothing to mitigate them.

You'd think that after quitting his job, Mark should've naturally gravitated towards something that would restore his lost attention.

But things are not that simple. Most people are not consciously aware of their important needs. It takes a good deal of introspection and experimenting before you can figure out what you really want to do.

Mark simply did not have the time for all that. His financial condition was growing worse.

While Mark was working in his new job, he decided to seriously *look* for his hidden talent in his free hours. He started experimenting again.

One day he tried his hand at stand-up comedy. When the audience roared with laughter at his quips, he finally figured out his life's passion. He was finally back to where he belonged- the center of everybody's attention.

Not only did he end his depression but he went on to become one of the top stand-up comedians in the country. Stand-up comedy made him happy and he wanted to keep getting better and better at it.

If your current activity doesn't satisfy your core need, whatever that may be, your mind makes you depressed so that you're motivated to seek the activity that does satisfy your core need.

It's important to note here that Mark was still not consciously aware of his need and didn't realize why he loved stand-up comedy so much. He overcame his depression pretty much accidentally.

At the peak of his success, he spoke to a group of wannabe comedians at a motivational seminar...

"We're all born to do something. I was born to be a stand-up comedian. You have to find out what you were born to do."

He had no inkling that he was actually satisfying an important childhood need. There's no such thing as "I was born to do this" or "I was born to do that". We love doing things because they satisfy our psychological needs.

It's important to note here that every case is unique. Not all youngest children crave attention or end up becoming stand-up comedians.

This was just one special case that we considered. Dozens of factors can work together to shape a youngest child's behavior in ways that can even make him not care about too much attention.

Now, let's move on to our next character- Shane.

"I'm Shane, an 18 year old student. I'm shy and hence find it very difficult to interact with people. I have no friends because I avoid social interactions as much as I can. I feel very sad, lonely and depressed. I've been depressed ever since I joined college about a year ago."

Here's a reply that he got...

Comment 1:

"Clearly, you're suffering from social anxiety disorder. There are several medications that you can take to relieve your anxiety such as Prozac, Zoloft, and Paxil. These will restore the serotonin levels in your brain and you'll feel better."

Shane visited a psychiatrist who prescribed him Prozac. He rushed to the pharmaceutical store and felt relieved as he held the small, yellow, plastic container of hope in his hands. This baby was going to put him out of his misery.

Not so fast. The medication seemed to work but as soon as he was off it, his anxiety and depression returned. During the same period he also experienced acute withdrawal symptoms.

The last thing he wanted was to continue popping pills for the rest of his life. He needed a long-term solution, not a quick fix.

The "medications" trap

This is by far the most common trap that depressed people fall into, because it's recommended by experts. Depression can only be ended by solving the underlying problem that's causing it.

I'm not saying that medications don't work. They do. But they only make you feel better for a while. When their effect fades, depression returns because the problem's still there.

It is claimed that medications restore the chemical levels in your brain that are disturbed by depression. However, a disturbed chemical balance might be an effect of depression, but it's definitely not its cause.

So when you're taking meds you're basically hiding/fixing the effect, not the cause.

There's no evidence whatsoever that a chemical imbalance in the brain 'causes' depression. It's just a correlation. But the media, backed up pharmaceutical companies, keeps pushing this message.[5]

On the other hand, stressful life events have been shown to have a substantial causal relationship with the onset of major depression.[6,7]

It's appalling how many so-called experts think that anxiety is a mental disorder. It's not. It's just another emotion.

Shane doesn't feel anxious in his home at all but only when he interacts with people. Since, he has to chronically meet other people in college, his anxiety is also chronically triggered.

This doesn't mean he's suffering from a mental disorder or has some sort of a brain defect because if Shane stays at home all the time than his anxiety will hardly get triggered.

Some people may be genetically predisposed to getting depressed but this doesn't mean fixing the brain chemicals will fix the root cause of depression.

This is the problem with the conventional approach to treating "disorders" with drugs. It barely takes into account the individual psychological make-up of a person and the specific environmental contexts that trigger various emotions such as anxiety.

While using meds may temporarily benefit those with severe depression, they're as good as placebos when it comes to treating those with mild depression.[8]

Antidepressants are also associated with increased risk of suicide and homicide attempts. Many patients are unable to stop these drugs because of intolerable withdrawal symptoms.[9]

Long story short, there are more cons than pros to using antidepressants and if you've truly understood how depression works you'll consider them downright useless.

Here's another advice that Shane received...

Comment 2:

"You need to change your attitude, Shane. Love yourself and think positive thoughts. Only by loving yourself will you be able to love others and appreciate their company. Change your thoughts, change your life."

"Sweet", thought Shane, "All I need to do is change my thinking and my depression will end" without being sarcastic.

So he trained himself to think positive thoughts. It worked for a while but his anxiety didn't end. He still faced problems interacting with others.

He was engaged in a constant battle of thinking positively that never seemed to end and strained his brain. He read positive and inspiring quotes every day to cancel out the negative feelings of his depression.

The positive thoughts that he superimposed upon his depression needed constant reinforcement so he downloaded some positive and motivational tracks that he could listen to everyday.

He did everything he could to 'stay positive' but his depression was still there and he knew it wasn't getting any better.

The "positive thinking" trap

To be clear, our thoughts do govern our emotions. There's no doubt about that. Emotions result from how we interpret (think about) our life situation and our surroundings.

We do have some degree of control over how we interpret our environment. In other words, though this interpretation mostly happens unconsciously, it can be consciously hacked into.

For example, if you feel bad because of an injury that leaves you housebound, you can change your emotions by changing how you interpret this situation.

You can tell yourself something like, "Now I can finally get all the time I need to read those books that I've always wanted to read but never got the time."

As soon as you start thinking this way, you may start to feel better because you have re-interpreted a negative situation in a positive way.

This is called re-framing and it's the very basis of what we call 'cognitive behavioral therapy' or CBT.

Why then is it a trap? Can it not help someone with depression?

The answer to that question lies in this question: "Can you constantly re-interpret your life situation for the rest of your life?"

If you can do that, go ahead, CBT is for you. You might be able to keep depression at bay. In fact, CBT has been proven to be quite effective in 'treating' anxiety disorders.

What I'm saying is that it's not a viable long-term solution. It might even come at a cost. Constantly re-interpreting a situation soon convinces your subconscious that you're deceiving yourself.

And self-deception can be particularly difficult to detect because it's usually unconscious and unintentional. It takes a good deal of courage to recognize that you're actually deceiving yourself.

If Shane stays at home thinking, "People suck. They're not worth my time. I should stay at home doing more important things" he surely will be able to feel better about himself but his anxiety problem will not end.

What he has done is re-interpret a negative situation (I can't handle people) as something positive (I'm better off without people). When he does this over and over, he'll soon realize he's deceiving himself because his anxiety will not have ended.

Realizing that you've been deceiving yourself can be painful. So he may claim even more vehemently that he doesn't care about anyone and doesn't care at all what others think of him.

There's a fine, almost non-existent line between positive thinking and self-deception.

How Shane ended his depression

Shane eventually sought help of a competent therapist who encouraged him to start interacting with people. It was hard at first but Shane was determined to conquer his anxiety.

He started meeting people, attended social events whenever he could and spoke in public whenever he got the chance.

He made many mistakes and felt really awkward at the beginning but he learnt from those experiences and improved. Within six months his anxiety reduced significantly and his depression ended.

Social anxiety was the root cause behind Shane's depression. His subconscious mind thought (and very accurately) that he lacked social skills and so made him avoid people. Over time this problem became bigger and bigger and led to depression.

Only when he proved his subconscious mind wrong by actively participating in social events was he able to end his depression.

It's all about changing your beliefs through experience, not empty positive thinking. When you change your beliefs, your thinking will automatically change.

CBT holds that if you change your beliefs by changing your thoughts, your emotions will change leading to a change in your actions.

In fact, it works more effectively in reverse. If you do actions that provide evidence to your subconscious, your beliefs will change leading to a change in your emotions and thoughts.

When you start out, you have weak beliefs to support what you're doing which is why it feels uncomfortable but eventually, with practice, you will solidify your beliefs.

No need to constantly think positively about your negative emotions. When you take the right actions, the negative emotions will simply disappear.

Finally, let's look at what our third character Anna had posted...

"This is Anna, a 24-year-old fashion designer. I was in a long-term relationship with a guy and we recently broke up after 5 years. I really loved him and still do but I know I can't have him back. I lie alone in bed all day trying to make sense of what happened and cry all night."

Comment 1:

"I suggest you put your past behind you and move on with your life. It's going to hurt for a while but time will heal everything. You just need to be patient."

Anna couldn't agree more. She knew time indeed was 'the great healer'. Even though her feelings were intolerable right now, she decided to stay calm till the storm passed.

Except that the storm didn't pass. It had been two months since the breakup and she still didn't feel any better. She eventually became sick and had to be hospitalized.

The "time heals everything" trap

Time doesn't heal anything on its own. Our life situations tend to change with the passage of time making us either forget about our problems or perceive them as no longer relevant.

If our life situation doesn't change much, doesn't resolve our problems and keeps reminding us of them, it wouldn't appear that time heals everything. Rather, it would appear it's making our problems worse.

Imagine yourself thirsty in a desolate desert on a hot summer's day. If you're stuck like this for days, time will not heal you. It will kill you.

Instead of waiting for time to heal things, had Anna taken the responsibility to change her life situation herself she'd be better off.

Sure, her life situation could have improved itself, but life is unpredictable and unreliable. And when you're depressed you can't rely on life to make things right.

A much better strategy would be to take deliberate action yourself so that you can end your depression. In the golden words of Dr House, "Time doesn't change things. Doing things changes things."

Comment 2:

"Anna, I understand how you feel. Make sure you don't ruin your relationships with people that do love you and care about you- your family members and friends. Try reaching out to them for support. Try not to shut yourself out."

Anna took heed and decided to spend more time with her family. But deep down she knew she wanted to be alone. So a conflict arose in her mind that stressed her even more.

She did enjoy spending time with her family but a part of her mind was begging her to be alone. Her family members and friends gave her all sorts of comfort and reassurance that improved her mood, but only temporarily.

Finally, to the disappointment of her family and friends, she confessed that all she wanted to do was be alone.

The "spend time with others" trap

Social support is effective only as long as it helps you eliminate the root cause behind your depression. Loneliness was not Anna's problem here, breakup was.

As mentioned earlier, depression's purpose is to force us to re-evaluate our life and make strategies to change our life situation. By spending time with her loved ones, she was only distracting herself and hindering depression's real purpose.

This is why her mind kept pulling her back and why she felt like what she wanted most was to be alone.

There's an important point to be noted here. Had her family and friends offered a viable solution to her problem, her depression *could* have ended. But they only repeated conventional advice such as "Get over it", "We're here for you", "Everything will be all right", etc.

Being close to our family and friends boosts our mood because it gives us a sense of security, but it doesn't necessarily solve the underlying cause of depression.

How Anna ended her depression

Thus far, we've been discussing relatively simple cases of depression. It's time to show you how complex depression psychology can get.

In her alone moments, Anna reflected over her life situation over and over but it didn't yield anything. Then it hit her that her previous boyfriend looked very similar to the one with whom she just broke up.

She decided to talk to a relationship expert about this, hoping to find a clue about what was going on.

Her previous relationship had lasted only a year because the boyfriend had to move to a new country permanently. A month later she had entered into this new relationship that lasted 5 years.

When the first breakup happened, she was devastated and couldn't bear the pain. She thought that the guy was perfect for her but life didn't quite agree.

She couldn't come to terms with fact that she had just lost her Mr Right but ultimately managed to get over it, or so she thought.

Her subconscious mind was like, "Not so fast, honey. We're not letting him go that easy."

So what did her subconscious mind made her do?

Did she force her ex-boyfriend to return?

Of course, not. That wasn't possible.

Her subconscious mind made her fall in love with the first guy that looked similar to her ex-boyfriend.

To the unconscious mind, similar-looking things are the same. We subconsciously associate facial features with personality traits.

For example, if your aunt who was very kind to you in your childhood had a round face, then you may automatically assume that all grown women with a round face are kind.

When Anna's subconscious noticed this new guy, it thought it had found Mr Right again. So, it forced Anna to fall in love with him.

And because she had already broken up with "him" once, her mind ensured that the bond be stronger this time so that the possibility of breaking up again is reduced.

Her mind was like, "Let's go grab him! We're not letting him slip away from our life again."

The result- she fell in love with this guy intensely and their relationship lasted five years. And when she broke up with him, it hurt intensely too.

For five years, her subconscious mind tried to convince her that this new boyfriend was "the one" that she had lost earlier. She overlooked his flaws and incompatible personality traits.

Ultimately, reality prevailed and pushed the two people apart.

Had the previous boyfriend been less than perfect, then this breakup wouldn't have been so painful. Or perhaps she wouldn't even have fallen in love with this guy in the first place.

When Anna became conscious of all these facts, she smiled. This deep awareness of the workings of her mind helped her see her depression objectively and gain a sense of control over it.

Her depression no longer had any power over her. She was ready to move on with her life now.

The power of awareness

Throughout this book, I've been reiterating that to overcome depression, you have to solve the underlying problem that is causing your depression.

But what if the problem cannot be solved?

Does that mean you remain stuck in depression forever?

No.

If your depression is the result of a problem that you *can* solve, the best strategy is to solve that problem.

If, however, there truly is nothing you can do to end your depression, you have to become *aware* of the fact that there's really nothing you can do about your depression.

That awareness itself then becomes the solution to your depression problem.

Take, for example, the death of a loved one. People feel great sorrow, pain, and depression when someone close to them dies.

Though this depression does force them to reflect on life, it's kind of useless because they *know* that they can't bring back the dead.

So they can reflect on their life situation as much as they want, but formulating a strategy to bring back the deceased would be ludicrous.

The mind eventually realizes that depression is not needed here and so they recover within a matter of days or weeks or months.

The closer the relationship the more time it takes to recover but ultimately the person *is* able to deal with this sort of depression and doesn't seek help.

Yes, there may be a deep sense of loss in their heart but their normal life tends to continue normally.

Becoming conscious of your unconscious mental processes is the first step in overcoming any psychological problem, including depression.

Once you understand what's going on, then you can figure out what you need to do. If there's nothing you can do, then the awareness that there's nothing you can do itself becomes the solution.

Anna couldn't do anything about her situation. She now knew that the guy she just broke up with wasn't right for her. Her mind had fooled her into thinking that he was.

Step-by-step procedure to getting over depression

1) Identify the life problem that's causing your depression

The quick way to do this is to recall what was happening in your life when depression hit you. What changed? What changed especially with respect to your career and relationships? What source of your happiness was taken away? What major loss did you suffer?

Monitor your thoughts and figure out what your mind is desperately asking of you.

When you've successfully identified the problem that's causing your depression, getting over depression becomes easy.

If multiple problems are causing your depression, then you'll need to identify and eliminate each one of them.

2) Make a plan to solve your problem

No, not in your head. Get a piece of paper and write it down. Write everything down- how you're feeling right now, why you're feeling this way and, what you'll do to get over it.

This is the most important step that is oft-repeated by self-help gurus and for good reason.

When you're done making the plan, you'll notice that your feelings will have greatly improved. When you write out your plan, your subconscious thinks you've actually begun solving your problem- that you're on the right track.

So there's no need for any more depression- you've finally listened to the message that your mind had so gotten tired of sending you. You've started working on changing your life situation.

3) Work on your plan

At this stage, you have two options: You can either forget about the plan that you made or you can start working on it. The ramifications of these two actions are very different as far as your mental well-being is concerned.

If you forget about your plan because you feel slightly better now, depression will return when you're reminded your unsolved problem.

You can again make a plan to trick your mind into making you feel better but this time your mind will trust you less because you didn't implement your plan the last time.

Still, your feelings will improve, but probably not as much the previous time.

When you do this over and over, your mind will eventually get desensitized and not trust your plans anymore.

A point may come when your depression becomes so severe that you won't be able to ease your feelings just by making a plan because you've conditioned your mind to believe that making a plan doesn't work.

But what if you decide to work on your plan as soon as possible?

Your depression will be virtually over and your mind will thank you.

What if the plan doesn't work?

If a plan doesn't work, bad feelings may return but you have nothing to worry about because you can always make another plan and work on that.

When one plan fails, you should immediately make another one and if that one fails too then you should make another one.

You have to move from failure to failure till you reach success. If you allow failure to stop you, your depression will return.

When your plan works and you solve your problem, your mind will trust your plans even more.

So, the next time you're depressed and you start making a plan your mind will be like, "This worked the last time. It'll probably work this time too."

Advantage of writing things down

When you write something down, it's immediately absorbed into the subconscious mind. The subconscious then works on the problem outside of your awareness.

This is why, when you write down a problem that you need to solve or a goal that you need to accomplish, you tend to get light bulbs and insights while you're consciously busy doing other, unrelated activities.

Your subconscious mind is working on the problem while you're consciously involved with other tasks.

As soon as your subconscious comes up with a solution, it shoots it into your consciousness awareness as an insight or an intuition.

You may even get insights for a solution in your dreams when you're asleep.

Writing things down and making a to-do list also has the added advantage of keeping you focused on the tasks that you need to do. I'm not just talking about conscious focus here, but also unconscious focus.

"Unconscious focus? What is that supposed to mean? I thought we focused using only our conscious mind?" you might be thinking if you know little something about psychology.

Ever noticed that you tend to work on tasks that you didn't even remember you had jotted down in your to-do list, only to find out later that you had?

That's what I'm talking about. It happens a lot to people who write their goals down and make a to-do list.

There are countless examples of people who write their goals down and then, years later, when they see the list, realize they unconsciously worked on the exact same tasks.

When you write a goal down, it's absorbed into your subconscious and floats just below your level of awareness. From there, it becomes easily accessible to your consciousness.

Your subconscious mind then provides you with ideas and insights related to this goal much more readily, orchestrating your conscious activities to attain this goal.

This is why many success coaches aggressively advise writing your goals down. It works. I'm not sure if typing on a screen has the same effect but writing with a pencil or a pen is on paper is very effective.

Final Thoughts

It's high time you began looking at depression with a rational, cause-and-effect type of mindset. It's not a chemical imbalance or a passing bad mood that happens for no reason. Depression always has a cause behind it that you need to work on removing, if you can.

Getting over depression is pretty much like removing a thorn that gets stuck in the sole of your foot. You can wish all you want for the pain to cease or pretend that the thorn isn't there but unless you remove that piece of devil, there will be no relief.

The usual narrative in self-help and wisdom traditions is that our thoughts shape our lives. I hope I've convinced you that, in truth, it's the other way round.

Our mental state is a reflection of our life situation. When life situation changes, mental state changes. You can work on changing your mental state all you want, it won't necessarily change your life situation.

But work on changing your life situation, and you'll see how your mental state changes accordingly.

"Change your thoughts, change your life" is a lie. Change your life and your thoughts will automatically change.

Many people have this rosy image of the future where all their hopes and aspirations, wishes and dreams, stand fulfilled; where they're never unhappy and depression doesn't touch their shadow.

It's a fool's paradise. It will never happen and no such future exists. There never will be a time in your life when you can just click your fingers and say, "Okay, from now on I'll never be sad, unhappy or depressed."

Realize that depression, worry, anxiety, and sadness are normal human emotions that are there for good reason. They may feel bad and sometimes intolerable but they're ultimately useful. One only needs to understand them and manage them properly.

The goal is not to avoid depression because that may not be possible. The goal is to face depression and overcome it, no matter how many times it strikes.

Believe it or not, the happiest people in the world are the ones that were once the most depressed. Depression showed them what was wrong with their lives, and then they corrected those things and felt immense happiness.

In other words, they dealt with depression the way it is designed to be dealt with. Not surprisingly, remission of MDD is associated with important life improvements.[10]

Being depressed is not a bad thing or something to be ashamed of. Unlike those who deceive themselves, depressed people are more in touch with reality. Depressed people are realists that just need a better understanding of their emotional state which is what I hope this book has succeeded in communicating to the reader.

"Pain and suffering of any kind, if long continued, causes depression and lessens the power of action, yet it is well adapted to make a creature guard itself against any great or sudden evil."

- *Charles Darwin*

Too bad Charles Darwin isn't alive and here with us today to write proper comments on online forums.

References

1. Rottenberg, J. (2014). *The depths: The evolutionary origins of the depression epidemic*. Basic Books (AZ).

2. Abramson, L. Y., Metalsky, G. I., & Alloy, L. B. (1989). Hopelessness depression: A theory-based subtype of depression. *Psychological review*, *96*(2), 358.

3. Andrews, P. W., & Thomson Jr, J. A. (2009). The bright side of being blue: depression as an adaptation for analyzing complex problems. *Psychological review*, *116*(3), 620.

4. Lehrer, J. (2010). Depression's upside. *The New York Times Sunday Magazine*, *28*.

5. Leo, J., & Lacasse, J. R. (2008). The media and the chemical imbalance theory of depression. *Society*, *45*(1), 35-45.

6. Kendler, K. S., Karkowski, L. M., & Prescott, C. A. (1999). Causal relationship between stressful life events and the onset of major depression. *American Journal of Psychiatry*, *156*(6), 837-841.

7. Hammen, C. (2005). Stress and depression. *Annu. Rev. Clin. Psychol.*, *1*, 293-319.

8. Fournier, J. C., DeRubeis, R. J., Hollon, S. D., Dimidjian, S., Amsterdam, J. D., Shelton, R. C., & Fawcett, J. (2010). Antidepressant drug effects and depression severity: a patient-level meta-analysis. *Jama*, *303*(1), 47-53.

9. Gøtzsche, P. C. (2014). Why I think antidepressants cause more harm than good. *The Lancet Psychiatry*, *1*(2), 104-106.

10. Harris, T. (2001). Recent developments in understanding the psychosocial aspects of depression. *British Medical Bulletin*, *57*(1), 17-32.

www.ingramcontent.com/pod-product-compliance
Lightning Source LLC
Chambersburg PA
CBHW050522290526
45786CB00007B/2658